HONDA GOLD WING

DARWIN HOLMSTROM

Whitehorse Press
North Conway, New Hampshire

Whitehorse Press books are also available at discounts in bulk quantity for sales and promotional use. For details about special sales or for a catalog of motorcycling books and videos, write to the publisher:

Whitehorse Press
P.O. Box 60
North Conway, New Hampshire 03860-0060

ISBN 1-884313-22-1

5   4   3   2   1

Printed in Hong Kong

Contents

Acknowledgements

This book is dedicated to Mitch Boehm, editor of *Motorcyclist* magazine, whose support helped make this project possible. I'd also like to thank the other folks at the magazine who helped me with this project: Kevin Smith, Greg McQuide, and Allison Soled.

The following people put tremendous effort into helping me get photos for this book: Pete terHorst, Ken Vreeke, Tim Carrithers, Clement Salvadori, Nick Hoppner, Mark Tuttle Jr., and Doug Jackson.

Fred Rau deserves a special thanks for sharing his Gold Wing expertise with me, as does Rick Bartz for his legwork. I'd also like to thank all the Wingers who let me photograph their motorcycles, as well as all the other folks who put an effort into making this book a reality. And I can't forget Dan and Judy Kennedy, Jack Savage, and Lisa Dionne at Whitehorse Press. And of course my wife, Patricia Johnson, who's tolerated me and my motorcycles for almost a dozen years now.

Introduction

Redefining the Motorcycle

The King of Motorcycles

Mention the words "touring motorcycle" today, and one bike springs to mind: the Honda Gold Wing. That's as true for non-riders as it is for riders. The Gold Wing is the universal currency for touring bikes, the standard against which all others are measured.

That wasn't always the case. Back in the mid-1970s, Harley-Davidson's Electra Glide was the "King of the Highway"—that is, if you believed everything you read on the Electra Glide's saddlebags.

The thing was, nobody, not even the fellows who designed saddlebags for the Harley-Davidson Motor Company, believed it. In those deepest, darkest days of AMF ownership, no one considered an unreliable, underpowered, overpriced anachronism manufactured by a bowling ball company to be the king of anything, except perhaps the driveway oil stain.

In the experimental days of the 1970s, no one was even certain what constituted a motorcycle worthy of that title. Of the several contenders for the crown, each fell short in some respects. Kawasaki's Z1 dominated all comers at the drag strip, but its handling left much to be desired.

Left Honda's Gold Wing defines the touring motorcycle concept for riders and non-riders alike.

Right Harley-Davidson motorcycles embodied cutting-edge style in the 1970s, but under AMF ownership, the company developed a reputation for poor reliability.

BMW's R90 provided strong competition, but its high price placed it out of reach for many riders. Suzuki, a company that has always shuffled to the beat of its own drummer, believed rotary engines would power the future king, but few outside the company shared their belief.

This industry confusion allowed Harley to continue selling the same basic machine it had been selling since the Great Depression. Like it or not, the Electra Glide was the only full-dress heavyweight touring show in town.

But all that was about to change. Half a world away from Harley's Milwaukee headquarters, Japanese engineers and designers were putting in overtime at Honda's Wako factory, creating not just the king of the highway, but the "King of Motorcycles," the Gold Wing. Like their counterparts the world over, Honda's design team didn't know what exactly constituted the king of motorcycles, but they did know the Gold Wing would be as good or better than any motorcycle ever built.

Top *Kawasaki's mighty Z1 was the fastest bike available when Honda introduced the Gold Wing. This example uses a Rickman frame and café-racer bodywork.*

Bottom *Italy produced great-handling bikes like this Ducati 900SS. The trick was to find one for sale outside of a few select metropolitan areas.*

Their confidence in their own abilities proved well-placed. With the 1975 Gold Wing, Honda produced the ultimate road bike of its day. It didn't handle as well as some costly European exotics and it was a tick slower than the Z1, but it was far more reliable and practical than the Europeans and much more sophisticated than the big Kawasaki. For most riders, especially U.S. riders who valued comfort more highly than their European counterparts, the Gold Wing was the ultimate motorcycle, the king its designers intended it to be.

"Real" Motorcycles

By 1975, the fact that such a machine came from Japan had only the faintest whiff of surprise about it. While some people were still suspect of all things foreign—enough people to keep Harley-Davidson busy selling 1930s technology, in fact—most enthusiasts accepted Japan as the motorcycle-manufacturing *wunderkind* of the world. They expected Honda's entry into the liter-class bike market to be a technological tour de force.

A decade or more earlier, it would have been unthinkable for a Japanese company to build a bike like the Gold Wing. In post-war America there were only two kinds of "real" motorcycles: big British parallel twins and even bigger American V-twins. If you wanted a back-road burner, you bought a British bike, a light, quick, agile machine that vibrated like crazy, leaked oil, and had a minimalistic electrical system that didn't work. If you wanted to get out and see the country, you bought a Harley dresser, a large, cumbersome, slow machine that vibrated like crazy, leaked oil, and had an extravagant electrical system that didn't work.

Even a resourceful motorcyclist could find few alternatives to the above scenario. BMW made expensive, quirky, brutally efficient motorcycles, but they were only available in small numbers in select metropolitan areas. The Italians made expensive, quirky, fine-handling sporting motorcycles, but characteristically showed absolutely no interest in actually selling their magnificently-designed motorcycles, so they weren't available anywhere.

Regardless of which option you chose, one thing remained constant: the image of the motorcyclist as an outlaw. The general public considered motorcycles instruments of Satan. Being a biker in post-war America, a country where people like Joe McCarthy and J. Edgar Hoover rubbed out nonconformism with iron fists, was a way of publicly aligning yourself against God, motherhood, and the American way.

The Japanese Revolution

Toward the end of the 1950s, odd little machines from Japan began popping up in the United States. By the early 1960s, little Japanese motorcycles with exotic features like oil injection and electric start were everywhere. High school and college students zipped around campus on bikes with weird, foreign names like "Honda" and "Yamaha." Even the most skeptical hard-core motorcyclist had to admit these fun little machines were well-engineered, but they still weren't considered "real" motorcycles.

Real or not, these non-threatening Japanese bikes paved the way for motorcycling's eventual acceptance by the general public. They were ridden by "the nicest people," as the famed Honda ad claimed. The leather-clad hoods who might someday ride into your town to drag for beers, rape your daughters, and destroy all you considered sacred and holy wouldn't be caught dead on such devices.

The engine displacement of Japanese bikes crept up, as did their public acceptance, but as long as they were relegated to toy-bike status, Harley-

Although it wasn't what the motorcycling press expected, Honda's new Gold Wing proved to be everything its designers had hoped for—the "king of motorcycles." (photo courtesy Rider magazine)

9

Prior to the Japanese motorcycle invasion of the 1960s, the only motorcycles widely available in the United States were big Harley tourers or British hot rods like this Triumph Bonneville.

Small-displacement, easy-to-ride-and-maintain Japanese motorcycles, like this Honda Benley, were promoted as fun, wholesome machines in Honda's famous "nicest people" ad campaign, and they opened motorcycling to an entirely new market segment.

Davidson and the British manufacturers saw no reason to worry. They didn't realize what they were up against until the mid-1960s, when Honda introduced the CB450. Although still in the small-displacement category, national dirt-track racers like Denny Kannenberg were putting the little Honda into the AMA winners circle, beating Triumphs and KR Harleys with nearly twice the CB450's displacement.

By the time the established manufacturers figured out what was happening, it was too late. Honda was already at work on its next big thing, the four-cylinder CB750, a bike that changed the face of motorcycling like no other machine before or since. Everyone expected Honda to capitalize on the success of the CB450 and produce a real motorcycle—that is, one with an engine capacity of 650cc or larger. Some even predicted a monstrous 750cc machine, but almost everyone expected it to be a parallel twin.

When the CB750 appeared sporting not two, but four cylinders, the motorcycling world lost control of its collective bodily functions. There had been fours before, first expensive, hot-running longitudinal in-line fours of the type built by Indian and Henderson in the earlier part of the century, and more recently in the exotic production street bikes produced by legendary Italian race-bike manufacturer MV Agusta.

But the CB750 was a four for the masses, a bike that combined Honda's growing reputation for quality with a level of performance previously unheard of in a production street bike. Honda had built a bike that could outrun even the fours from MV Agusta, and at a fraction of their cost.

The motorcycling public had come to expect anything from a company that could build such a bike. When it came time for Honda to take the next logical step and enter the big-bore motorcycle market, motorcyclists anticipated something great. They didn't expect the Gold Wing.

When Honda introduced the CB450, the rest of the motorcycling world realized that Japan was serious about building motorcycles.

The New Breed

In 1975, America was in the middle of the biggest motorcycle boom it had ever seen. The huge numbers of babies born just after World War II were entering their twenties, and they not only had money, they were restless. In other words, they represented a dream demographic group for a company selling motorcycles. Since they generally bought the fastest, most powerful bikes available, performance came to dominate motorcycle development. Every new motorcycle introduced was marketed as the fastest in its class.

Uncharacteristically, the Gold Wing wasn't the last word in outright performance. It was fast, but Kawasaki's Z1 was faster. Honda's new masterpiece confused more than a few magazine writers, especially European scribes, who decried the Wing's complexity and weight. In its January 1976 issue, England's *Bike* magazine proclaimed the Gold Wing a "Two-Wheeled Motorcar."

Arguably, the Honda CB750 (shown here in full Rickman café-racer form) had a greater impact on the history of motorcycling than any other motorcycle before or since.

When Motorcyclist *writer Bob Greene saw the Gold Wing prototype at Honda's 1974 dealer and press show in Las Vegas, complete with frame-mounted fairing, he realized he was looking at the future of motorcycle touring. (photo courtesy* Motorcyclist *magazine)*

Honda's new machine confused many in the press who expected the new bike to be a Z1-beating hot rod. Mike Wright owns this 1975 Gold Wing. (photo by Adrienne Warren, courtesy Wing World*)*

But a few insightful writers understood what Honda had accomplished and realized they were witnessing the birth of a new class of bike. "And here, by God, is a tourer, unblurred and brilliantly focused," wrote *Cycle* magazine in the very first full road test of the Gold Wing published in its April, 1975 issue.

Motorcyclist's Bob Greene had an even more prescient vision of the Gold Wing's future impact when, in that magazine's December 1974 issue, he wrote that "Honda's ultimate touring masterpiece" would "take off on a trip all its own, pioneering a sophisticated concept yet untouched but soon to be pursued by those destined to follow the leader."

Initial public reaction didn't back up Greene's prediction. Honda sold just 5,000 Gold Wings in 1975, but any concerns over the slow sales of Honda's king of motorcycles were laid to rest as the Gold Wing caught on in succeeding years. However, the Wing's impact extends beyond mere sales success. The Gold Wing took off on its own trip, as Greene prophesied, defining the luxury touring motorcycle, a category Honda has dominated for over a quarter of a century.

Perhaps more importantly, the Gold Wing rewrote the image of the motorcyclist held by the general public. With this bike, Honda had created a new breed of biker: the Gold Winger. In turn, Wingers would break down the long-standing myths about outlaw motorcyclists, proving once and for all that you really do meet the nicest people on a Honda.

First came the Gold Wing. Then came the Wingers, motorcyclists like Mike Hoff and Diane Heberholz who prove you really do meet the nicest people on a Honda.

Chapter 1
Project 371

The Ego Bike

Honda didn't build the Gold Wing to meet any perceived need expressed by the motorcycling public. Prior to the introduction of the Gold Wing, most motorcyclists didn't even realize there was a need to be fulfilled. Rather, the Gold Wing was about corporate prestige. Corporate ego drove development of the bike more than customer demand. To understand why Honda built the Gold Wing, it helps to understand the manufacturing culture that spawned the bike. The first twenty-five years of the Japanese motorcycle invasion were a time of technological one-upmanship, with one Japanese company leap-frogging ahead of the next. The Gold Wing was meant to put Honda back at the front of the race.

In the early 1970s, the category of long-distance touring rider didn't exist as we know it today. A few grizzled riders chugged around the country each summer aboard antiquated Harley-Davidsons, veteran motorcyclists who could rebuild their unreliable machines alongside any road, at night, with nothing but an adjustable wrench and a Zippo lighter. An even smaller group of European enthu-

Left The Gold Wing wasn't designed specifically with the touring market in mind, because when Project 371 was first initiated back in 1972, that market did not exist as we know it today. Rather, the Gold Wing was more of a corporate status symbol for Honda to show the world what the company was capable of building. (photo courtesy World's Motorcycles News Agency)

siasts strafed U.S. highways on expensive BMW and Moto Guzzi motorcycles—reliable machines for the most part, but should they break down in any burg between the two coasts, the rider might have to wait so long for parts to arrive that he or she could expect to be a local by the time the bike was once again up and running.

A few exceptions to these stereotypes began to emerge, as young, limber riders immune to the aches and pains that come with age began to explore the country riding inexpensive Japanese motorcycles. The best of these, the four-cylinder bikes from Honda and Kawasaki, made halfway-decent traveling companions, but poor suspensions, thinly-padded seats, and maintenance-intensive chain final-drive systems made them less-than-ideal touring mounts.

Prior to the Gold Wing, no manufacturer had attempted to build an ideal touring bike, in large part because no one realized there was a market for such a bike. Honda discovered that market as much by accident as by any forward thinking on the part of its engineers and management. The introduction of the Gold Wing reflected an attempt to best Kawasaki more than it represented a bold move into an untapped market. Honda wanted to recapture the bragging rights for building the world's greatest motorcycle.

Just a few short years earlier, Honda claimed undisputed ownership of those rights. Honda's CB750 provided a level of performance previously available only on a racetrack, and it did so at an astoundingly inexpensive price. This bike propelled Honda to the forefront of motorcycling in a far more visible

When Honda introduced its Gold Wing, Harley was still using the same basic technology it had been using since it introduced the Knucklehead in 1936. Jerry Staggeberg (pictured) owns this Knucklehead.

A resourceful motorcyclist with plenty of cash could purchase one of BMW's fine touring motorcycles, like this 1976 R90S, provided he or she could find a dealer within 500 miles of home.

manner than even the company's historic racing victories of the 1960s. Scribes coined a new phrase to describe the mighty 750: "Superbike." The impact the machine had in the United States was so great that for a while, the word "Honda" became synonymous with "motorcycle."

It would be more than half a decade before Honda introduced its next large-displacement streetbike, and in the fast-moving motorcycle marketplace of the 1970s, six years equaled several lifetimes. Other companies cashed in on Honda's success, introducing machines that made the CB750 appear tame by comparison. BMW punched out its 750cc boxer twin engines, creating the R90 series bikes. Suzuki introduced 750cc liquid-cooled, two-stroke triples. The biggest blow to Honda's corporate ego came in the form of Kawasaki's 900cc, double overhead-cam, four-cylinder Z1.

Out on the road, the wicked-fast Z1 made Honda's "little" 750 look slower than a box of rocks. At a stop, the situation didn't improve much for the Honda. Not only was the Z1 the fastest production

motorcycle a person could buy, it also looked modern, with its twin-cam engine and sleek bodywork. In comparison, the old-fashioned Honda looked downright frumpy.

The M1

The folks at Honda didn't appreciate Kawasaki's Z1 demoting their 750 superbike to also-ran status, and they set about correcting the situation as soon as they learned of Kawasaki's activity. In December, 1972, at Honda's Wako engineering center in Japan, a design team headed by Shoichiro Irimajiri, who had worked on Honda's fabled six-cylinder Grand Prix racing motorcycles, was given a rather straightforward task: complete internal project 371. The assigned goal of Irimajiri and his crew was nothing less than to design and build the ultimate motorcycle.

Irimajiri and company came up with a bike unlike any the world had ever seen—or likely even imagined—a shaft-driven grand tourer powered by a 1470cc, single overhead-cam, liquid-cooled flat-

Many riders modified their Japanese motorcycles for touring, although judging by the extended fork and apehanger handlebars, this fellow had his idioms crossed.

Kawasaki's big four-cylinder bikes, shown here in 1000cc form, ruled stoplight drag racing in the mid-1970s.

six. Dubbed the M1, it weighed a svelte 484 pounds. Carburetion consisted of a single downdraft two-barrel carburetor and the intake manifold was heated by engine coolant. The M1 engine cranked out a mere 80 horsepower, not that much more than Kawasaki's 900cc four-cylinder engine, but power delivery was infinitely smoother than the buzzy Kawasaki's.

Irimajiri's team had created the M1 primarily to explore the possibilities of engine development. At the time, Honda didn't have a workable driveshaft system of its own, so a BMW unit was borrowed to expedite the process. It would take nearly three years of hard work to develop a reliable shaft-drive system, partly because the founder of the company, Soichiro Honda, insisted that engineers could not advance a current design until they'd mastered the most basic elements of the design. Thus Honda's engineers were often forced to design a system or process from scratch.

Mr. Honda himself was somewhat skeptical about the M1. He believed the public would reject motorcycles over 750cc, and he had a predilection toward air cooling, since he generally favored simple systems over more complex ones. In his excellent book, *Gold Wing: The First 20 Years,* Ken Vreeke wrote that when Mr. Honda first saw the M1, he said it "looked like a bat." Then, to the dismay of the engineers, he took it out for a ride. Vreeke writes:

"He hopped on the big machine, started it, and rode out into the darkness. Technicians and engineers peered anxiously after him, imagining a disaster for which they would surely be responsible. In due course he returned safely, parked the machine, remarked that it was 'pretty good,' and went home."

History has shown us that the basic design of the M1 was indeed "pretty good." The architecture of the engine, the horizontally-opposed, multi-cylinder layout, proved to have two tremendous unforeseen benefits: a low center of gravity and a centralization of mass. These benefits made the bike feel much lighter than its actual weight of nearly 500 pounds would suggest, in turn allowing designers and engineers to create a much larger motorcycle than their customers were accustomed to riding. In large part, these unexpected bonuses made possible the modern heavyweight touring motorcycle.

As good as it was, the M1 was never intended to be a production motorcycle. The flat-six engine was too long to be packaged using existing frame geometry, forcing the rider's feet too far rearward and creating too long a reach to the handlebars. Besides, the bike was a bit much for the motorcycling public to accept at that time. The M1 was an exercise in self-definition for Honda. It forced engineers and designers to look beyond the limits of conventional thought, to tear down any barriers to creative thinking. Honda's production motorcycle would have to be something just a bit simpler, however. It would have to make do with a mere four cylinders.

The Gold Wing

Toshio Nozue, the engineer responsible for the CB750 project, led the team for the next phase of development. Nozue's team worked frantically at Honda's Tochiga test facility, work that resulted in the original Gold Wing prototype.

It was not easy work. The Gold Wing incorporated several systems that, while not firsts in the mo-

Although originally conceived as a design exercise to test the boundaries of the impossible, Honda's original six-cylinder prototype proved to be a vision of the future. For the M1, Shoichiro Irimajiri's team simply used a driveshaft pilfered from a BMW. For the production Gold Wing, such borrowed ideas would not be tolerated within Honda. (photo courtesy American Honda/Vreeke & Associates)

torcycle industry, were firsts for Honda. The previously-mentioned developmental problems associated with the shaft-drive system provides a good example. It took years to perfect the system. Yoicho Oguma, head of the group assigned to test the new bike, complained that the drive shaft broke on a daily basis.

Carburetion also proved to be a challenge. Unlike the M1, the production Gold Wing would use a quartet of downdraft carburetors. Honda's inexperience with liquid-cooling on motorcycles led to some serious problems, because the hot air stream from the radiator disrupted the carburetion process. This was partially solved by moving the engine air intake above the hot stream of radiator air, but it took two years to perfect the radiator and coolant plumbing layout.

Daunting as the technological challenges were, Nozue's crew rose to meet them. In the process, they improved on several systems. The shaft drive they devised proved to be more reliable and require less maintenance (that is, after Honda added an external grease fitting in 1976) than did the BMW system. Positioning the fuel tank beneath the seat, originally done to make room for the carburetion and air-intake system, added an extra bonus of improved weight distribution, enhancing the low center of gravity and centralized mass of the flat-four engine design.

Nozue and company encountered a problem when trying to design an engine-transmission package similar to the ones used by BMW and Moto Guzzi. When the transmission was grafted behind the flat, longitudinal, multi-cylindered engine, as Shoichiro Irimajiri's team had done with the M1, the package proved to be too long. To solve this, Nozue's designers located the transmission underneath the engine, much like a modern front-wheel drive automobile.

No other touch illustrates the ingenuity of Nozue's team like the dual-use alternator, which

For the production version of Honda's king of motorcycles, the company decided to go with something a bit less shocking than the M1. (photo courtesy American Honda/Vreeke & Associates)

doubled as a contra-rotating flywheel. The alternator rotated in the opposite direction of the crankshaft, so that in addition to providing electrical current, the inertia of the rotating armature canceled the torque reaction inherent in engines with in-line crankshafts.

This system has been the cause of some speculation concerning electrical problems over the years (see Appendix A), because it requires the alternator to spin at a steady speed, regardless of the bike's electrical need. The unneeded electricity produced by the Gold Wing's alternator is shunted back into the frame and dissipated as heat through an electronic valve. This could be viewed as a step backward from the excited-field alternator Honda introduced on its CB750 in 1969, a system that only produced the amount of electricity the bike needed, and thus less excess heat, but the Gold Wing's alternator needed to spin at a steady speed to function as an anti-torque device. In practice, it has worked quite well.

Nozue's team experimented with other innovations, too, such as fuel injection, automatic trans-

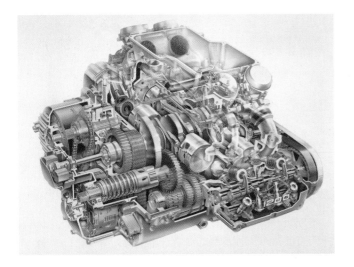

Top right Honda seemed as confused as everyone else when it came to marketing their new bike. (photo courtesy American Honda/Vreeke & Associates)

Top left Designing all the new systems for the sophisticated, four-cylinder, liquid-cooled, shaft-driven Gold Wing proved a daunting challenge. (photo courtesy American Honda/Vreeke & Associates)

Bottom Nozue's team located the transmission beneath the engine, automotive-style. (photo courtesy World's Motorcycles News Agency)

missions, hydraulic centerstands, and anti-lock brakes, but the available technology was simply too crude to be practical at the time. Besides, the new machine already had enough technological innovation to scare the relatively conservative motorcycle community.

What Is It?

Mastering the technology of the bike was difficult, but perhaps the biggest challenge was trying to figure out what the Gold Wing was supposed to be in the first place. The specifications of the original Gold Wing, first shown in prototype form at the Cologne Motorcycle Show in Germany in October, 1974, show Honda's confusion about how to market the bike.

The portly bike (635 pounds, wet) featured a liquid-cooled flat four driving the rear wheels through a driveshaft and a 60.5-inch wheelbase, features that indicated the bike was meant for long-distance touring. Yet the power-delivery characteristics of the 999cc engine, which made its peak power of 80 horsepower at a lofty 7500 revolutions per minute and propelled the Gold Wing through the quarter mile in under 13 seconds, indicated this was the Z1-beating hot rod the world expected. The triple-disc

Honda and the motorcycle press may have been confused about the Gold Wing's mission statement, but owners knew exactly what to do with their new machines: ride them.

brakes and thinly-padded saddle also hinted of sporting pretense.

For months, the motorcycle press had been buzzing with rumors of the next big thing from Honda, ranging from reports of a punched-out version of the CB750 to some sort of monstrous, liquid-cooled, shaft-driven V6. The Gold Wing fell somewhere between those two extremes, a compromise machine meant to appeal to the broadest audience possible.

The motorcycling press appeared just as confused about the new Honda as the company itself.

Some testers raved about the bike, others didn't understand it. Generally, U.S. scribes gave a more favorable impression than did their European counterparts.

Honda and the press may not have had a clear idea of what the Gold Wing was, but the people who bought Gold Wings knew exactly why they had done so: to cover the maximum amount of distance in the minimum amount of time, and to do so in as comfortable a manner as possible. The Gold Wing was the ultimate two-wheeled mileage disposal unit.

Chapter 2

The Touring Bike

The GL1000

Upon unveiling the new Gold Wing, Honda's publicity machine kicked into high gear, touting the Gold Wing as "the ultimate motorcycle."

Note that Honda didn't promote the Wing as the ultimate "touring" motorcycle, or the ultimate "sporting" motorcycle. The folks at Honda honestly believed the new Wing could be all things to all riders.

The Touring Bike

The buying public harbored no such misconceptions. Without Honda to direct them in the proper usage of the new bike, customers were initially slow to bring Gold Wings home from dealerships. But most of the 5,000-odd riders who purchased Gold Wings in 1975 soon realized what they had acquired: the finest long-distance, two-up touring motorcycle then available.

Opposite page
Although it would never find favor with the sporting crowd and become the all-purpose machine its creators intended, the Gold Wing found a home with touring riders, especially those in the United States.

Left
When they introduced it in the fall of 1974, Honda considered the Gold Wing a do-it-all kind of motorcycle. (photo courtesy American Honda/ Vreeke & Associates)

The GL1000 may have been the best touring bike of its day, but it had yet to achieve perfection. That would come later.

While touring accessories enhanced long-distance comfort and convenience, they amplified the inadequacy of the Gold Wing's suspension.

The GL1000 may have handled poorly compared to top-notch European sporting machinery, but when compared with its Japanese contemporaries and the offerings from Harley-Davidson, the Gold Wing acquitted itself well.

A Gold Wing sitting in a driveway acted as a beacon, calling its owner to the open highway. (photo courtesy Paul Johnson)

No one is certain who, exactly, was the first U.S. rider to purchase a Gold Wing, but it would be safe to bet that before he'd burned through a couple of tanks of gas, he'd made a trip to his nearest dealer to purchase an aftermarket fairing, most likely accompanied by a set of saddlebags and a more comfortable seat.

While sport-oriented riders stayed away from the Wing in droves—in fact, they ridiculed the portly new bike—riders who liked to ride farther than the nearest cafe or bar quickly made the Gold Wing their own.

Right from the start, owners knew their brand-spanking-new Wings had legs, and that these bikes wanted to get out on the road and go somewhere. The eerie smoothness of the drivetrain urged the rider to keep going long after the ride was supposed to end. The exhaust note from the flat four, which *Cycle* magazine described as "a muted whisper, much like a 912 Porsche with a standard muffler," insistently, almost subliminally instigated the rider to go out for a ride and not come back. The seamless competence of the Wing opened up entirely new possibilities for motorcycle travel.

Good, But Not Perfect

Honda's new flagship was good, perhaps the best motorcycle available, but it wasn't perfect. In themselves, most of the flaws in the new machine didn't amount to much, but the long distances people traveled on their Gold Wings served to amplify those flaws. Nothing points out a motorcycle's deficiencies like a string of back-to-back 750-mile days in the saddle.

In some ways, the imperfections took the form of minor annoyances, trade-offs necessary to gain the benefits of new systems. Riders discovered the new liquid-cooled Wing took a lot longer to warm up than did older, air-cooled motorcycles. The shaft-drive system traded messy, time-consuming chain maintenance for the quirky handling characteristics caused by the driveshaft, which fed throttle input back into the chassis, resulting in abrupt, up-and-down suspension motion when opening and closing the throttle.

Other problems with the new Honda were entirely of Honda's own making. Some contemporary scribes complained about the Wing's handling. The main culprit was excess weight—at 647 pounds wet, the Gold Wing was second only to Harley's lumbering 780-pound Electra Glide—but other factors played a role in the bike's less-than-stellar handling.

Like many Japanese motorcycles of the time, the Gold Wing came with fairly low-grade suspension components, even by the standards of the day. The springs were too hard at both ends, while the damping was too soft, producing a ride that was both harsh and poorly-controlled over rough pavement. In his review for *Bike* magazine, Bill Hayden complained about both the suspension and the frame design, which Hayden thought exemplified the tendency of Japanese designers to "indiscriminately bend tubes around various bits that happen to get in the way" without considering possible compromises to the integrity of the frame and adverse effects on the handling.

Certainly the suspension and handling characteristics of the Gold Wing left much to be desired, but this was also true of most of the Wing's competition. Riders accustomed to the laser-sharp precision of European sportbikes found the GL lacking, but riders used to the harsh ride of Harley-Davidsons or the rubbery suspensions found on most Japanese machines found the Wing's handling above average.

Above *Honda may have thought the Gold Wing could serve the dual role of sportbike and touring bike, but the buying public knew the new Wing was a tourer, plain and simple, and they wasted no time outfitting their bikes as such.*

Right *When Honda introduced the Gold Wing, the only motorcycle company that offered luggage and a touring fairing was Harley-Davidson, a firm no competitive manufacturer wanted to emulate at the time.*

The Aftermarket to the Rescue

The most obvious shortcoming of the Wing was its lack of any form of luggage or protection from the elements. Honda's decision to sell the GL1000 without any type of fairing or luggage did not come as a surprise to anyone, since Japan had yet to sell a bike that came equipped with anything other than the most minimal bodywork. In 1975, only a few small European manufacturers offered motorcycles with standard-equipment fairings, exotic machines like Ducati's 900 Super Sport. The only manufacturer that sold a motorcycle equipped with a touring fairing and luggage was Harley-Davidson, a company whose lead no right-thinking motorcycle company would consider following in 1975.

Perhaps Honda viewed the inclusion of a touring fairing as the first step down a slippery slope. First a fairing, and before you knew it, cast-iron, air-cooled, push-rod, V-twin engines would propel the company's state-of-the-art motorcycles. No, Honda decided, best not to travel down that particular path.

At the time, Honda was very much an engineering-driven company. It didn't build bikes to meet the demands of consumers. It simply built the best bikes it could conceive, then assumed consumers would show their appreciation by buying those bikes.

In a way, that approach worked with the Gold Wing. Sales soon approached a respectable 25,000

Left *Note the distinctive triangular shape of Vetter's luggage system.*

Above *In addition to his signature fairings, Vetter built and sold a popular line of aftermarket luggage. Note that the top case on this example is not a Vetter, but rather the trunk from Harley-Davidson's Tour-Pack system.*

Vetter

Craig Vetter shaped the future of touring motorcycles in the 1970s like no other single person. With his line of fairings, the most famous of which was the Windjammer series, Vetter literally defined how a touring motorcycle should look. Those fairings were so influential that to this day, some people still call frame-mounted fairings "Windjammers," or sometimes simply "Jammers."

Craig Vetter first came to fame in 1969 when Don Brown commissioned him to redesign the BSA Rocket 3, a motorcycle whose perceived ugliness was helping to drive the troubled English firm into receivership. By the time Vetter's design was ready for production, BSA had ceased to exist, but Triumph, BSA's sister company, was still limping along, so Triumph produced Vetter's design as the 1973 Hurricane. This bike influenced styling trends for the next decade.

Following the success of the Hurricane, Triumph commissioned Vetter to redesign its Bonneville TT. Based on Gene Romero's 1970 AMA Grand National Championship-winning Triumph race bike, the design was ready for production in 1974, but by that time Triumph was too far down the road toward oblivion and incapable of producing any new designs.

In addition to building and selling what was to become the most famous aftermarket fairing of all time, Vetter found time to race, and in 1975 he campaigned a Rickman Kawasaki throughout the AMA amateur road-racing season. This experience left Vetter with the desire to market his own motorcycle design.

In 1980, Vetter introduced his Mystery Ship, based partly on Reg Pridmore's 1978 AMA Superbike Championship-winning Kawasaki KZ1000. Using KZ1000 components, Vetter constructed a high-performance motorcycle with a one-piece gas tank, seat, fairing, and number plate. Vetter only sold 10 of these expensive ($10,000), custom-built machines, not exactly setting the motorcycling world on fire, but his design, with its enclosed bodywork, did predict the direction future sportbike design would take.

Bikes that came with integrated touring equipment from the factory, like Honda's Interstate and BMW's R100RT, foretold the downfall of aftermarket suppliers. Seeing the writing on the wall, Vetter sold the Vetter Corporation and began pursuing other ventures, but not before selling over half-a-million of his trademark fairings. ∎

The most famous Vetter Windjammer fairing of all time may have been the one mounted on Prince's Honda in the film "Purple Rain," here being held by John Bones, an employee of Sport Wheels, the Minnesota-based salvage yard that currently owns this piece of memorabilia.

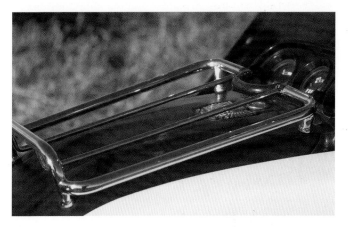

Clockwise, top left The shape of Vetter's Windjammer became the shape of touring motorcycles for more than a decade.

Top right Nothing protected a 1970s motorcyclist from the elements like a Vetter Windjammer.

Above The GL1000's fake gas tank afforded riders a novel place to mount a luggage rack.

Left No GL1000 Gold Wing was complete without a Vetter Windjammer fairing, the fairing that came to define touring motorcycles in the 1970s. This bike uses Vetter lowers designed specifically for the Wing.

units per year. Customers appreciated the Wing's many virtues, but they still didn't want a naked touring bike, regardless of what Honda thought. Few Gold Wings survived long in the nude outside the rarefied atmosphere of Honda's corporate confines. Most owners mounted aftermarket fairings soon after purchasing their new Gold Wings, and fairing manufacturers sold almost as many fairings as Honda sold Gold Wings. No one sold more fairings than Craig Vetter, whose Windjammer series defined touring motorcycles in the 1970s.

Adding aftermarket fairing and luggage made the Gold Wing much better suited for long-distance travel, but it also highlighted the shortcomings of the bike's suspension. Assuming most riders would travel solo, Honda calibrated the suspension of the original GL1000 for a fairly light load, never dreaming Gold Wingers would choose to travel two-up more often than not, putting additional strain on the already-overtaxed suspension. Throw in the weight of a fairing and some heavily-loaded luggage, and the poorly-suspended Gold Wing was in over its head.

Again, the aftermarket provided a fix. Air shocks, fork braces, and stiffer fork springs found their ways onto Gold Wings nearly as fast as did Craig Vetter's fairings.

Serious Design Flaws

Some problems with the Gold Wing, such as lack of weather protection, cheesy suspension, and an uncomfortable seat, were easily remedied by the aftermarket. Other problems inbred into the big bike's design proved more difficult for customers to correct. The capacity of the underseat fuel tank, optimistically rated at five U.S. gallons, proved woefully inadequate, especially given the Wing's voracious appetite for distilled petroleum. Perhaps Honda thought that their painful seat would encourage frequent fuel stops, but once an owner had mounted a comfortable aftermarket saddle, those

frequent stops became an even bigger pain than the thinly-padded stock seat.

To warn the rider of impending doom, Honda blessed the Gold Wing with an electronic fuel gauge, but the inaccurate nature of this gauge almost made it more of a bother than a help. In his infamous *Bike* review, Hayden described the gauge as "worse than useless—it just frightens you by reminding you how rapidly the juice is burning."

Given the design of the underseat tank, increasing fuel capacity to extend the bike's range proved a nearly-impossible task. Some European owners went as far as to convert their bikes to the use of LP gas, but these ungainly, power-robbing, and ugly

Rather than whine about their bikes' shortcomings, Gold Wing owners simply modified their bikes to meet their needs. (photo courtesy of Paul Johnson)

conversions (they required mounting a large LP tank on the bike) were never very popular. Most people just lived with the short cruising range.

Some flaws in the equation were the direct result of Honda's indecision over whether to market the Gold Wing as a sportbike or a tourer. The inadequate fuel capacity provides a good example of this indecision. Honda tried to give the bike enough capacity for long-distance travel, but stopped short of actually achieving that goal for fear the added weight would push the big bike over the top for the sporting crowd.

Wing Wins Over Touring Crowd

But the bike was already over the top for the sporting crowd. Then, as now, the Wing appealed to a mature crowd more interested in making the next state by dinner time than in strafing each apex at the maximum possible velocity. Generally speaking, Gold Wingers are more interested in providing a comfortable perch for their spouses than in shaving off a few tenths of a second from their lap times. A typical Gold Wing rider differed as much from a typical rider of a Ducati sportbike as a Ducati rider differed from the rider of a Husqvarna motocross racer. There was some overlap to be sure, but not enough to turn a motorcycle like a Gold Wing into the all-purpose machine its creators envisioned.

The new GL1000 found a home in the United States, where riders had different needs than their European counterparts. U.S. riders had much more open space to cover, and the new Honda was the best bike yet for covering those spaces in as short a time as possible. They were accustomed to having the wind knock the hell out of them while crossing vast sections of the country. The Wing's low center of gravity and centralized mass made it supremely stable on trips across the windy plains. U.S. motorcyclists wanted that, and they were willing to take care of the suspension shortcomings, uncomfortable seats, and lack of touring accessories them-

The retuned engine of the 1978 Gold Wing made less top-end power, but more power in the mid-range, where a rider could use it. (photo courtesy American Honda/Vreeke & Associates)

selves. They made the GL1000 a sales success, and helped Honda sell nearly 21,000 units in the second year of production.

Honda began improving the Wing almost as soon as it went on sale. In 1977 Honda installed a set of touring handlebars that sat about 2.5 inches higher than the originals. Honda replaced the universally-despised waffle-pattern grips that adorned most Honda handlebars in the early-to-mid 1970s with more comfortable, smooth rubber grips. "It boggles the mind," *Cycle World* wrote in its July 1977 test. "Imagine buying a new Honda and not having to immediately replace the grips." Honda also attempted to improve the seat, but the results drew mixed reviews.

For 1978, the company went quite a bit farther in its Gold Wing updating program. Engineers actually went inside the engine to tinker around with the powerband, making it better suited to the needs of a heavyweight, long-distance touring bike. By using smaller carbs, shortening the valve timing, and increasing the spark advance, the altered Wing engine had a lower top speed and produced slower

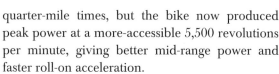

quarter-mile times, but the bike now produced peak power at a more-accessible 5,500 revolutions per minute, giving better mid-range power and faster roll-on acceleration.

The new bike had a more complete set of gauges located in a pod on the fake gas tank, where the fuel gauge had been located on the previous bike. Unfortunately, anyone mounting a tankbag would block his or her own view of the gauges.

Honda updated the new bike's appearance by swapping a high-tech set of modular pressed-metal wheels for the traditional wire-spoked units. Known as "ComStars" in Honda vernacular, these wheels were used on many Honda motorcycles in the late 1970s and early 1980s, until they were replaced by simpler (and presumably cheaper-to-produce) cast wheels in the mid-1980s.

Gold Wing Redefines Honda

The Gold Wing had an impact on Honda that went beyond mere sales numbers. In many ways, it changed the way Honda did business. The fact that owners radically modified Honda's king of motorcycles as soon as they bought them was not lost on the company.

Although the most extensive changes to the Gold Wing yet, the 1978 improvements were just Band-Aid fixes—and the press knew it. Bikes from other manufacturers had been improving, and the Gold Wing was losing all the comparison tests conducted by the magazines. Of the 1978 Wing, *Cycle* magazine wrote: "In its heart and soul the GL1000 still says 1975."

Honda knew this, too, but the company that introduced the original Wing in 1975 was not the same company that introduced the 1978 version,

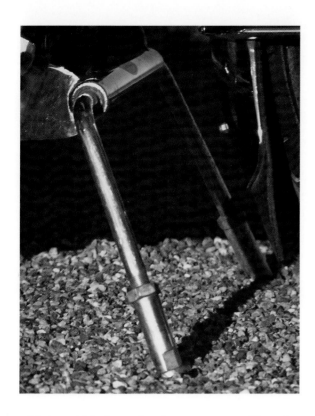

Far left *For 1978, the GL1000 included a more complete set of gauges. Unfortunately, their location rendered them useless should the rider choose to use a tankbag.*

Middle left *Honda replaced wire-spoke wheels with more modern-looking ComStar units in 1978.*

Left *Ride-off stands like this were popular accessories for Gold Wings in the 1970s.*

with its cobbled-together improvements. The relationship between Honda and its customers had changed during that time. Visionaries within the company had seen the difference between Honda's corporate vision of the ultimate motorcycle and the buying public's vision of that same bike. Honda's experience with the Gold Wing forced it to become a customer-driven company instead of an engineering-driven company. By the time Honda introduced the 1978 GL1000, it was well on its way to producing the bike its customers really wanted.

Chapter 3
Full Dress

Time for a Rethink

Touring riders had needs peculiar to their style of riding. They wanted more mid-range power for passing traffic and climbing hills, especially when their bikes were loaded with luggage and hauling passengers—or even pulling trailers, a completely-unforeseen practice that developed around the Gold Wing. For these tasks, the Wing's performance was in the wrong place with its original, high-strung 999cc powerplant, even after the powerband tinkering of 1978. As the 1970s wound down, the original GL1000 rapidly approached its expiration date.

By 1979, bikes from other manufacturers had completely surpassed the Gold Wing in every objective measure of performance. Still, GL sales remained strong, due to the appeal of the basic design. Other bikes may have gone faster, handled better, and provided more rider comfort, but they still couldn't match the smoothness inherent in the liquid-cooled, flat-four engine, nor, for the most part, its proven reliability.

The CBX

The first step in the Wing's evolution was to relieve the GL of its multi-purpose role. If customers refused to accept the Gold Wing as a superbike and only saw it as a touring machine, then Honda would develop it as a grand-touring motorcycle.

Left *The Interstate version of the Gold Wing took the touring bike concept to a new level. (photo by Clement Salvadori)*

That meant Honda would have to provide customers with a more sporting superbike, so Honda began developing what it thought would be the most sporting motorcycle ever unleashed on the public. In 1978, Honda introduced its six-cylinder CBX, a magnificent but flawed machine. Development had begun in 1976, before Honda had internalized the mistakes they'd made with the original Gold Wing. When development of the CBX began, Honda still worked within the build-it-and-the-buyers-will-come paradigm. With the CBX, its 24-valve six-cylinder engine a mechanical marvel even today, Honda built the most technologically impressive motorcycle it could conceive, regardless of whether the buying public wanted such a bike or not.

Unfortunately, while it was a spectacular showcase of engineering prowess, the CBX was not a very good motorcycle. Its high center of gravity and non-centralized mass hindered the big, complex machine's handling, as did the bikes excessive weight and the overall width of its six-cylinder engine. And the complexity didn't equate with capability. For all its mind-boggling technology, other simpler, cheaper bikes were faster, handled better, and were a lot less work to maintain.

A Grand Tourer from the Get-Go

Flawed or not, the CBX made possible the most critical aspect of the Gold Wing's evolution. Freed of the need to fill both superbike and touring roles, engineers were able to pursue development of the Wing as the world's grandest touring bike.

When Honda's six-cylinder CBX took over the role of superbike, it freed the Gold Wing to fulfill its destiny as the ultimate touring motorcycle.

Simpler, cheaper motorcycles, like Suzuki's GS1000S, were better sportbikes than the cumbersome CBX.

One of the values Soichiro Honda instilled into the company bearing his name was the need to learn from mistakes. Mr. Honda once described his life as "nothing but a series of mistakes, a series of failures, a series of regrets." But he credited those failures for his ultimate success. "Success can be achieved only through repeated failure and introspection," he said. "In fact, success represents one percent of your work and results from the 99 percent that is called failure." Honda definitely learned from the failure of the CBX, as well as from the shortcomings of its original GL1000. In developing the second-generation Gold Wing, Honda swallowed its pride and, instead of engineering a motorcycle simply to show off their own technological capabilities, it used those capabilities to build the bike its customers wanted.

By the time the GL1100 was released for the 1980 model year, Honda knew what its customers wanted. Engineer Shuji Tanaka, who took over as the large project leader for the Gold Wing in 1978, made use of an odd phenomenon that sprang up around the Gold Wing: the worldwide rallies and riding clubs devoted to the Wing. These were especially prevalent in the United States, and Tanaka traveled around the United States on a Gold Wing, attending rallies and meeting Gold Wing riders, learning first hand what owners wanted from their bikes. He used the information gathered during his travels to help develop the motorcycle Honda's customers demanded.

The new Gold Wing was that motorcycle. With the GL1100, Honda addressed all of the perceived shortcomings of the original Gold Wing. Some solutions proved more effective than others, but the new bike was an improvement in every area.

Refining the Concept

Although an all-new bike, the GL1100 was very much a Gold Wing, recognizable to the bike's legion of fans. For the second generation GL, Honda adopted a strategy of refinement. With the CBX carrying the superbike banner, Honda didn't feel the need to start from scratch with the new Wing, and kept its basic layout. A water-cooled, flat-four engine still powered the shaft-driven behemoth, although that engine was much improved over previous versions.

Honda took the most obvious and sensible route to gaining more power by bumping engine displacement to 1085cc. To cope with the added power, the drivetrain was reinforced from the crankshaft through to the transmission output shaft. The crankshaft was strengthened to address the failure of some early GL cranks when they were run flat out for extended periods. A new clutch design attempted to address another problem with the original Wing. While adequate for normal riding, the GL1000's clutch tended to fail when abused, and seldom lasted for more than a half-dozen drag strip runs when being tested by magazine editors.

Tanaka's team didn't just pursue raw horsepower in their rethink of the GL powerplant. They knew that the quality of the power the engine provided was as important to touring riders as the quantity. Toward that end, they engineered the new engine to provide better mid-range power and improved roll-on performance. They accomplished this by using 1mm smaller carburetors (30mm, down from 31mm in the 1979 Wing). These changes increased torque enough for Tanaka's crew to revise the valve timing and lift, changes which, along with more radically-profiled cams, increased top-end performance as well as mid-range power.

Tanaka's team didn't just stop their engine-improvement campaign at a simple overbore, either. New pistons bumped up the compression ratio, and a new, .25-inch wider primary chain featured a more positive tensioner to eliminate crankcase noise.

Honda listened to the criticisms of Gold Wing owners, and the GL1100 of 1980 went a long way toward rectifying any shortcomings. (photo courtesy World's Motorcycles News Agency)

Thicker brakes improved stopping power. Plastic valanced fenders and aluminum ComStar wheels helped bring overall weight down. (photo by Clement Salvadori)

The new, more accurate fuel gauge now resided up in the instrument pod along with the temperature gauge. (photo by Clement Salvadori)

The dimpled valve cover distinguished the GL1100 engine from other four-cylinder Gold Wing powerplants. (photo by Clement Salvadori)

Unlike touring packages offered by other manufacturers, the Interstate's fairing and luggage didn't have a single visible bracket or hose clamp. (photo by Clement Salvadori)

These changes resulted in a significantly more powerful bike all through the rev range. The GL1100 *Cycle* magazine tested for its January 1980 issue turned in a quarter-mile time of 12.47 seconds at 107.39 miles per hour.

Stabilizing the Beast

A lack of high-speed stability plagued the original Wing. While not much of a problem in the United States, which had a draconian 55-mile per hour speed limit at the time, the high-speed weave of the GL1000 created much distress in Europe, where some highways had no speed limits at all. A tendency to weave at high speeds helped the Gold Wing earn a reputation as a truly-terrifying machine to ride on Germany's Autobahn.

To help stabilize the GL, Honda lengthened the wheelbase and improved the suspension. Rede-

signing the frame had been part of the plan from the moment Honda selected Tanaka, a frame designer with bikes like the CBX to his credit, as the large project manager. He would later develop the frames for such bikes as the 750 Magna and 750 Saber V-fours. Tanaka's team stretched the GL1100 wheelbase to 63.2 inches, an astounding figure for 1980. In addition to making the bike more stable at high speeds, this stretch increased passenger room.

Few aspects of the original Wing came under as much criticism as the original suspension, making a redesign inevitable. The suspension on the new Wing used air pressure to control damping and compression. Owners could adjust the suspension in both the fork and the rear shocks by adding or subtracting air.

To further stabilize the beast, Honda increased the diameter of the fork tubes from 37mm to

Every piece of luggage was perfectly color-matched on the Interstate. (photo by Clement Salvadori)

The Interstate's fairing set new standards for rider protection. (photo by Clement Salvadori)

39mm. Although puny by today's standards, these were huge forks back in 1980. Wider tires, now of the tubeless type, graced the ComStar wheels, making the new Wing even more stable at speed. These changes effectively cured the GL of its uncouth high-speed behavior, but just to be safe, engineers added a six-pound iron weight to the steering head. Honda realized that buyers of expensive 640-pound luxury motorcycles generally don't appreciate 110-mile per hour tank-slappers.

With more power and better handling, the new Gold Wing was likely to see more high-speed use than the old Wing, so Honda upgraded the brakes as well as the rest of the suspension, mounting larger, thicker discs both front and rear to help slow the bike down.

More Improvements

Honda tackled a variety of other problems with the new Wing, too. An electronic ignition with both centrifugal and vacuum advance replaced the troublesome contact breaker points found on the GL1000. The GL1100 featured other electrical improvements, too, such as a more powerful three-stage alternator to handle any electrical accessories owners might use. To facilitate the use of such accessories, the bike had a built-in accessory socket.

The new stepped seat was more comfortable than the flat saddle it replaced. Valanced fenders not only looked more stylish, they did a better job protecting riders from road spray than the old chrome units. Honda also raised fuel capacity a whopping .2 gallons, bumping it to 5.3 gallons, and replaced the previously useless fuel gauge with a more accurate instrument.

Although not nearly enough of an increase in fuel capacity, this small increase, when combined with the smaller carbs and more efficient electronic ignition, did improve the Wing's range. Also helping to increase the bike's range was the fact that at 637 pounds wet, the GL1100 now weighed 13 pounds less than the original GL1000, in spite of being a significantly larger motorcycle. The GL1100's designers cut weight in a number of ways, such as using aluminum rather than steel for the inserts on the new, wider ComStar wheels.

In addition to the new fenders, Honda introduced a few other stylistic changes. The valve covers of the new Gold Wing sported distinctive dimples between the cylinders, making the GL1100 easy to distinguish from earlier (as well as later) versions. The new GL no longer had fold-out panels on the sides of the fake gas tanks. In its December 1979 issue, *Motorcyclist* attributed this change to the fact that the panels would interfere with the optional Interstate fairing that Honda planned to offer for its new flagship.

Dead-Center Perfect

The motorcycle magazines loved the new Gold Wing, especially in the United States. *Motorcyclist* raved about the new "super smooth" engine, saying it "no longer feels peaky, and it pulls strongly from low rpm." The new air suspension received similar praise. In its April 1980 test of the new Wing, *Cycle World* wrote: "The suspension is simply the best there is." *Cycle* marveled at the new bike's comfort in its January 1980 test, noting that "while gazing at car passengers a realization hits you: you're more comfortable than they are."

Even the traditionally anti-Wing European press had to admit a grudging respect for the new Gold Wing. In January, 1981, *The Biker* wrote: "Within the limits of its ground clearance, [the GL1100] handled remarkably well. The suspension really gives a comfortable ride." Even *Bike* was forced to admit, after a high-speed trip across Europe, that "the Honda acquitted itself remarkably well as a Eurotripper considering its origins as a Yank interstate troller." Although they called the GL1100 "The Incredible Bulk," describing it as "oversized" and "overpowering," *Motorcycling* magazine had to admit that "despite the machine's size it is virtually well balanced. On motorways the Wing is a gem."

Motorcyclist concluded that the Gold Wing "has finally become the interstate cruiser it always promised to be." *Cycle* concurred, stating: "The Gold Wing is, after five years, close to dead-center perfect for its intended purpose."

The Interstate

Honda introduced the naked GL1100 to rave reviews, but bigger things were soon to come, although at first the press didn't quite grasp the significance of what Honda had in mind. *Motorcyclist* editors mentioned the optional "Interstate package" Honda planned to offer, and gushed about what an opulent and complete touring package it would be—and, of course, they were right. It would certainly be unlike anything the motorcycling world had ever seen. But the Interstate was much more than a "package." The Interstate was a new motorcycle. In fact, it was a new direction in motorcycling.

By 1980 there was no shortage of touring packages for motorcycles. In addition to the offerings from the plethora of accessory companies like Vetter and Krauser, the motorcycle manufacturers themselves offered accessory frame-mounted touring fairings and hard luggage that included both saddlebags and a trunk. The vast majority of these fairings and bags were universal units that mounted on a variety of bikes, held in place by a motley collection of brackets, U-bolts, and hose clamps.

Like its fairing, the Interstate's luggage became the industry standard for quality. (photo by Clement Salvadori)

Recognizing that the passenger often had as much influence on the decision to buy a bike as did the rider, Honda's Interstate coddled the co-rider. (photo by Clement Salvadori)

Not only was the Interstate luxurious, it was rugged, too. Many of them are still on the road, in all kinds of weather.

BMW upped the touring-bike ante when it introduced the R100RT in 1978. This bike, with its aerodynamic fairing and lowers sculpted around its air-cooled boxer twin engine, set new standards in the seamless integration of touring accessories. Harley-Davidson, a company on the brink of extinction, surprised the motorcycling community by bringing out its remarkably advanced Tour Glide. In addition to an integrated frame-mounted fairing and complete luggage, including a large trunk, the Tour Glide used an Erik Buell-designed frame that isolated the quaking of the old Shovelhead V-twin engine from the rider with a complex system of rubber donuts and adjustable Heim joints.

Neither of those bikes really made much of an impact on the motorcycling public. BMW was still the same low-volume manufacturer of high-quality-but-eccentric motorcycles it had been since Max Fritz first bolted together the first R32 boxer twin in 1923, and Harley was still stumbling toward oblivion. Even more than BMW's R100RT, Harley's Tour Glide was viewed more as an oddity than as a functional motorcycle.

The Interstate version of Honda's new Gold Wing fit in the category of BMW's R100RT and Harley's Tour Glide. Its bodywork, the frame-mounted fairing that featured an adjustable windshield, the saddlebags, the touring trunk, all blended in with the GL1100 in a way that could only have been achieved with pieces designed side-by-side with the machine itself. Nowhere could you find ugly brackets, hose clamps, and bolted-on supports. Rather than looking tacked on, the Interstate looked finished. This smoothly-integrated feel was further enhanced by the perfectly color-matched paint on every piece of the bike.

The Interstate offered a host of luxury features never before available from a motorcycle manufacturer, although Gold Wing owners had been adding such features to their own bikes for years. GL buyers could purchase optional stereos with built-in in-

Top *Honda began manufacturing Gold Wings at its Marysville, Ohio, plant in 1980. (photo courtesy American Honda/Vreeke & Associates)*

Bottom *Motorcycle assembly proved so successful in the United States that Honda expanded, adding an engine plant in Anna, Ohio. (photo courtesy American Honda/Vreeke & Associates)*

Touring riders had spoken: "More is better." Honda responded with the Aspencade in 1982.

tercom systems and cassette decks. Many details, like fairing-mounted headlight adjusters, came as standard equipment. Recognizing that spouses often have as much input into the purchase of a luxury touring bike as does the rider, Honda tailored many of the Interstate's features and accessories to meet the passenger's needs.

Born in the U.S.A.

1980 marked the year in which the Gold Wing finally fulfilled its promise as a touring bike, but that year also marked another milestone for the Wing.

On May 1, 1980, the first Gold Wing rolled off of Honda's assembly line in Marysville, Ohio. Soichiro Honda believed in building bikes in their intended market. Since Honda exported 80 percent of GL production to North America, the Gold Wing was the logical bike to build in the United States. The fact that the Wing had the highest profit margin of any motorcycle Honda built also may have influenced the decision.

Honda chose to build its first U.S. plant in Marysville, Ohio, in part because the chosen location was next door to the Ohio Transportation Research Center, a publicly-owned facility that boasted a 7.5-mile test track. Even though the Marysville plant was specifically designed to produce the Gold Wing, it produced CBX and CR250 motocross motorcycles in 1979, the facility's first year of operation, primarily because Honda was still developing the Interstate version of the GL1100.

Honda took a risk when it decided to build a factory in the United States during the late 1970s. At that time, the quality of many American-made products, especially U.S.-built motor vehicles, was abysmal. Harley-Davidson had so many difficulties with its suppliers that it often had to substitute inferior components just to keep shipping motorcycles to its dealers. As a result, some Harleys arrived at the dealerships in such poor condition that they needed engine rebuilds right out of the crate. Chrysler's vehicles were held in such low esteem that the company was forced to seek a government bailout to keep its doors open. Although not in as dire financial straits as Chrysler, General Motors engaged in similar actions during that time. These practices led to the production of such low-quality vehicles that the label "Built in the U.S.A." had little consumer appeal in the late 1970s.

To avoid quality control problems that could destroy Honda's growing reputation for building the most reliable vehicles on the road, Honda went to great effort to export its manufacturing philosophy to Marysville along with its motorcycles. The company even sent many new employees to Japan for training before production of motorcycles began. The gamble paid off—the motorcycles (and later cars) built in Marysville were at least as good as the Hondas coming out of Japan. The venture was so successful that Honda even built an engine-manufacturing plant 40 miles down the road from Marysville, in Anna, Ohio. Like the Marysville plant, that facility was initially designed to produce Gold Wing engines.

Honda's Aspencade offered features unheard of in a motorcycle, including an on-board air compressor. (photo courtesy World's Motorcycles News Agency)

The Aspencade

The Interstate was an immediate hit, and dealers around the world quickly sold out their first year's inventory. Honda wanted to drop the standard bike from the lineup and concentrate on production of the Interstate model, but the loud complaints of the aftermarket prevented them from carrying out that plan. Not that such complaining did them much good. There was no way equipment designed to work in a variety of applications—equipment designed around the bikes it was to be used on rather than being designed in conjunction with those bikes—could compete with the seamless Interstate. The aftermarket could pressure Honda into building standard Wings, but it couldn't pressure people into buying those bikes.

Honda had a winner on its hands, and it was clear what direction future development of the bike would take. For 1981, Honda made some incremental improvements to its flagship touring bike, adding a polycarbonate windshield that was more scratch-resistant than the original, and all models benefitted from advanced self-canceling turn sig-

nals that were controlled by speed, steering angle, and duration. In addition to the optional AM/FM radio with intercom, options included a voltmeter, quartz clock, and ambient air temperature gauge.

Honda made some across-the-board improvements for 1982, such as adopting the vented disc brakes from the CBX and mounting a set of powerful dual-piston calipers to grip them. Suspension engineers also lightened the steering by using smaller diameter wheels, the front going from 19 inches to 18 inches and the rear going from 17 inches to 16 inches. The saddlebags became even more waterproof with a lid redesign, but Honda had something a lot bigger than incremental improvements in mind. It planned to take the touring bike to the next level.

As luxurious as the Interstate was, it was downright frumpy when compared to the new Gold Wing model Honda unleashed in 1982: the Aspencade. Named after a popular American touring rally, the Aspencade offered riders a higher level of luxury than anyone had ever seen, or likely even imagined. With its two-tone metallic brown or

The Aspencade took its name from a popular U.S. touring rally.

two-tone metallic silver paint, the new model looked the part of the world's most opulent motorcycle, and it lived up to those looks. All the luxury items available as options on the Interstate, accessories like a stereo with built-in intercom system, came as standard equipment on the Aspencade. Buyers could even get a CB radio. Of course, the Aspencade had an upgraded alternator to power all this extra equipment.

The standard-equipment item that garnered the most attention, however, was the on-board air compressor. Riders could use the compressor to adjust pressure in the Aspencade's air suspension by manipulating a rather complex set of controls mounted in a pod on the fake-tank cover. The ignition switch needed to be in park to add air to the suspension. Air could be removed from the suspension at any time. This system helped push the Aspencade's wet weight up to 766 pounds, and its retail price to a staggering $5,698. It also helped slow quarter-mile performance to around 13.5 seconds at 98 miles per hour.

Honda's new Aspencade floored the world's motorcycling community. Journalists' excitement about Honda's new flagship nearly caused many scribes to search their thesauri looking for new superlatives to describe the magnificent machine confronting them. *Motorcyclist's* Dexter Ford came up with perhaps the most unique description of the Aspencade when he wrote (with apologies to Kenneth Graham) in that magazine's June 1982 Aspencade test:

"As if in a dream he found himself, somehow, seated in the rider's seat; as if in a dream, he pulled the lever and swung the Aspencade round the yard and out through the archway, and, as if in a dream, all sense of right and wrong, all fear of obvious consequences seemed temporarily suspended. He increased his pace, and as the bike devoured the street and leapt forth on the high road through the open country, he was only conscious that he was Ford once more, Ford at his best and highest, Ford the terror, the traffic queller, the lord of the lone trail, before whom all must give way or be smitten into nothingness and everlasting night."

Enough riders thought the Aspencade was worth $5,698 to make the bike a sales success.

Chapter 4

Responding to Competition

The Aspencade Era

If Gold Wingers ever design a new calender to re-place the Gregorian version currently in use, 1982 will become year one, and everything prior to that will be backdated as Before Aspencade, and every-thing following year one will be considered After Aspencade. Honda's Aspencade forever changed riders' expectations of what constitutes a luxury touring motorcycle. After motorcyclists gained ac-cess to the level of equipment found on the Aspencade, few were willing to go back to the rela-tively spartan bikes of only two years earlier.

Honda continued its process of gradually im-proving the Gold Wing line in 1983, implementing across-the-board changes. Cheaper-to-manufacture cast wheels replaced the ComStar units. Engineers added a fork brace as standard equipment, mimick-ing an aftermarket item long popular with Wing riders. The improved front-end stiffness comple-mented a stiffer rear end, achieved through the use of a stronger box-section swingarm. A removable rear fender section facilitated rear tire changes.

For 1983, Honda's TRAC (Torque Reactive Anti-Dive Control) braking system, which in-creased fork compression damping during braking, allowing suspension designers to use softer spring rates. 1983 also marked the first year of unified braking on the Wing. Honda's unified braking sys-tem operated in much the same way as the system Moto Guzzi had used since the mid-1970s, with the

Opposite page

With its hydraulically-adjusted valves, the new Gold Wing was as close to maintenance-free as a motorcycle could get.

Left

Honda used digital instruments on a Gold Wing for the first time with the 1983 Aspencade.

foot pedal operating the rear brake and the right front disc brake and the handlebar lever operating the left front disc brake. In practice, this system was more advanced than Moto Guzzi's, utilizing a proportion-sensing valve that kept the rear brake from locking up under hard use. Even so, the system never received universal acclaim. Some people loved it, while others hated it. Most, however, found they could at least tolerate it.

The most obvious change for 1983 was the use of a liquid-crystal display on the instrument panel of the Aspencade. Although the instruments were still fork-mounted, as they had been on all previous Gold Wings, the instrument pod on the Aspencade contained a collection of high-tech electronic gauges and digital readouts rather than the simple round dials found on earlier bikes.

The 1983 Wing benefitted from a number of other changes designed to improve both rider and passenger comfort, further broadening the Wing's two-up riding capabilities. Designers moved the luggage rearward to increase passenger room, and made the passenger footpegs adjustable to accommodate a wider range of inseam lengths. The softer suspension provided a smoother ride, and the Wing

Honda modified the infamous shin-bashing Gold Wing case guards, but the new versions still victimized many a leg bone.

used taller gearing to lower engine rpm at cruising speed. Raising gearing eight percent did lower engine speeds, but it also hurt roll-on performance, necessitating a downshift for passing below speeds of 60 miles per hour. Had this been like any other year in the GL's nine-year life span, this change would have been hardly worth noting. But 1983 wasn't like any other year. It was the year the Gold Wing finally got some serious competition in the luxury-touring market.

Competition

The early 1980s were a remarkable time in motorcycle development, in part thanks to a sales war being waged in Japan. Yamaha decided to knock Honda from the number one slot in motorcycle sales, and began a contest of one-upmanship that led to a dizzying variety of ever-improving motorcycles from both Yamaha and Honda.

Yamaha got the jump on Honda in the burgeoning cruiser market in the late 1970s. The success of Yamaha's Special series, lightly-modified standard bikes that edged ever closer to the Harley-Davidson cruiser look, gave Yamaha momentum going into the 1980s. Honda responded by introducing cruiser-style bikes of its own, in turn forcing

Regardless of how much better the seat was on each new Gold Wing, riders still preferred aftermarket units.

Yamaha to respond back, each new bike a shot fired over the bow of the competing manufacturer. When Yamaha introduced the Virago V-twin cruisers, Honda responded with its Shadows. When Honda built a complex, underachieving turbocharged motorcycle, Yamaha responded in kind. It was only a matter of time before Yamaha countered Honda's dominance of the luxury-touring market. Yamaha introduced its Venture and Venture Royale touring bikes in 1983.

The new Yamahas came on the scene at a time when the Gold Wing was vulnerable. Although it was just three years old, by 1983 the GL1100 had already become a somewhat dated design. A number of niggling problems manifested themselves in the Wing, such as the engine guards on the Interstate model that earned a reputation for destroying riders' shins. Honda redesigned these guards in 1982 to make them less intrusive, but they still took their toll.

Compared to Yamaha's new Venture, the bodywork of the GL1100 looked tacked on. (photo by Clement Salvadori)

In 1983 the unthinkable happened—Yamaha's Venture captured the luxury touring crown from the Gold Wing.

The GL1100 seat had always received mixed reviews. While *Cycle* described the seat as "a luxurious, plastic-bottomed giant that looks—and feels—like a king's drawing room chair," *Motorcyclist* described that same seat as "the least comfortable GL seat ever, because its contours, surface pattern and stiff foam didn't quite harmonize." Even after the firmness, height, and contours of the seat were modified in 1981, *Motorcyclist* said the seat's shape "did not fit the average American buttocks."

Heat buildup in the cockpit area also plagued the Gold Wing, especially in full-dress form. Referring to the heat buildup, England's *Bike* magazine said, "The Aspencade is still the best split-level grill I've yet ridden."

In spite of being the bike's most publicized feature, the Aspencade's on-board air compressor did not escape criticism. Because air could be let out of the system without the ignition key, vandals could release air from an unattended bike's suspension. This not only made a vandalized Aspencade unsafe to ride, it could potentially lead to the bike falling over while parked on its sidestand. Righting a bike that weighed 764 pounds was no easy feat. Adjusting the suspension to the proper settings was a tricky proposition, thanks to the fidgety nature of the air compressor controls. "We like the idea of the compressor," *Motorcyclist* wrote, "but it does need some debugging." Honda did debug the air compressor on second-year Aspencades, requiring the ignition to be in the "on" position for suspension adjustment and moving the controls from the tank-top pod to the fork crown.

The improvements Honda incorporated in 1983 weren't enough. For the first time ever, the Wing wasn't the best touring bike on the market. The motorcycling press was in near-unanimous agreement that Yamaha's new Venture Royale deserved that honor. As *Cycle Canada* wrote in its October 1983 issue, the Venture "has more power, handles better and is more comfortable than the Aspencade." The Yamaha was much more powerful than the Gold Wing throughout the entire powerband. *Cycle Canada* said the Venture, with its powerful V-four engine, made the Aspencade feel "like a 550" in comparison. Although a bit top heavy at walking speeds, the Venture also trounced the GL1100 in handling, thanks to its superior

ground clearance. With the exception of parking-lot maneuvering, the new Yamaha bested the Aspencade in all objective measures of performance.

Even if the Venture hadn't outperformed the Aspencade, it may have beaten the Honda on sheer style alone. Yamaha's big V-four looked the part of a modern touring bike. While the Gold Wing was designed as a naked bike first, its touring fairing and luggage still an afterthought, the Venture was designed as single unit—there was no naked version. The Venture's fairing flowed seamlessly into the rest of the bodywork, its side panels integrated with its fairing panels, and its luggage blending into its side panels. *Cycle Canada* wrote: "The Aspencade is still a Gold Wing with a number of accessories attached to it, and styling suffers as a result."

Scribes thought the Venture marked the end of the Gold Wing's long tenure as the king of the luxury-touring bike market. "Perhaps the Venture will gather its own group of touring cultists with a taste for heavyweight touring at a new standard of engine performance and handling," *Cycle Canada* prophe-

While the GL1200 bore a strong family resemblance to its ancestors, beneath the skin was a whole new machine.

sied. Perhaps it would have, all other things being equal. But Honda didn't get to be the world's premiere motorcycle builder by letting all other things remain equal.

The GL1200

The all-around competence of Yamaha's Venture energized Honda, who wasted no time in responding. But rather than mimicking the sporty Venture and building a sport-oriented tourer around its potent V-four engines, Honda elected to continue the Gold Wing's evolution as a luxury tourer, focusing on increased long-distance comfort.

The GL1100's replacement, the GL1200, attracted more attention for similarities to its predecessor than it did for differences, at least until closer examination. While the basic lines and architecture of the GL1100 remained, the GL1200 featured a new engine, with only the fuel and oil pumps carried over from previous versions. The new bike also had a new frame, wheels, fairing, luggage, seat, and suspension. "Same name," *Cycle* proclaimed on the cover of its February 1984 issue, "same dress, but . . . a whole new bird."

Once again engine capacity had been increased for more power. The new Wing displaced 1182cc, mostly due to a longer stroke. Larger intake valves and more aggressive cams combined with the increased displacement to help the new engine crank out more power, but any increase in power output was offset by taller gearing and the weight of the new bike, which, at 789.5 pounds, outweighed the original Wing by 142.5 pounds. The GL1200 required a downshift or two for fast passing on two-lane roads. *Motorcyclist* recorded a 13.2 second quarter-mile time at 98.5 miles per hour. That was a tick slower than the 12.92 second 104.52 mile-per-hour quarter time turned in by *Cycle's* original GL1000 back in April of 1975. It was also slower than the 1982 Aspencade tested by *Motorcyclist,* which turned in a 12.99 second quarter mile at 99.11 miles

The 16-inch front wheel deserved much of the credit for the nimble handling of the GL1200.

per hour. In the contest everyone was watching, it was trounced by Yamaha's Venture, which *Cycle Canada* ran through the quarter mile in 12.64 seconds at 106.6 miles per hour.

Clearly raw speed did not constitute an important part of the new Wing's mission statement. Rather, the GL1200 engineering team, once again headed by Shuji Tanaka, focused on putting the power where touring riders most needed it—in the mid-range. The new engine's torque peaked 500 rpm lower than the GL1100 mill, contributing to both better roll-on performance and lower cruising rpm.

A Nimble Wing

By now, Honda had realized that touring riders placed less emphasis on quarter-mile times and more on handling and comfort, areas where the new Wing made huge strides.

Honda built a naked version of the GL1200 in 1984, more to appease aftermarket suppliers than to meet customer demand. Few people bought the standard Wing, and it was dropped after just one year. (photo courtesy of Rider magazine)

Although the GL1200 featured the best Gold Wing seat yet, most owners still turned to the aftermarket.

Most testers thought the GL1200's electronic dash was too busy. What would they have thought about this custom upholstery?

The GL1200 possessed remarkably nimble handling for a bike weighing the better part of 800 pounds. A redesigned frame deserved much of the credit for the Wing's new-found agility. A stiffer chassis and bigger 41mm fork tubes contributed to the GL1200's road manners, as did moving the engine ahead 2.5 inches in the frame to put more weight on the front wheels. The engine was angled up three degrees in the front to increase cornering clearance. The swingarm was lengthened more than two inches, but overall length increased only two-tenths of an inch. Honda used stiffer springs at both ends, lowering compression damping, but increasing rebound damping, and increased suspension travel in the rear.

A decrease in wheel diameter, from 18 inches to 16 inches in the front, and from 16 inches to 15 inches in the rear, contributed the most to the new Wing's improved agility. By decreasing both unsprung mass and centrifugal force, 16-inch wheels lightened steering considerably, a huge advantage on a 790-pound motorcycle. *Cycle* wrote in its January 1985 test of an Interstate: "The shift to a 16-inch front and a 15-inch rear may have been the most important change, giving the GL a nimbleness previously unknown to the touring fraternity."

Despite its improvements, the GL1200 couldn't keep up with Yamaha's Venture when it came to high-speed handling. The new Wing still wallowed around during hard cornering, and cornering clearance was still limited. But, as Honda well knew, most American touring riders valued handling versatility over high-speed handling, and in this way the new Wing excelled. It didn't have to beat the Venture in every performance contest to beat it on the showroom floor. In some areas, the Gold Wing only needed to be competent. "The Aspencade hasn't the clearance of the Yamaha Venture," *Cycle* wrote, "but now, at least, the GL has *enough*."

The GL1200 showed the world just how waterproof motorcycle luggage could be. (photo courtesy World's Motorcycles News Agency)

A New Level of Convenience

In addition to taking the touring bike to a new level of agility, Honda's 1984 GL1200 took the breed to a new level of convenience. The original GL1000, with its belt-driven overhead cams and shaft drive, had started the trend toward low maintenance, and the GL1100 had taken it to the next step with electronic ignition, but the GL1200 proved to be the lowest-maintenance touring motorcycle on the market.

Taking cues from its successful Nighthawk and Shadow series, Honda made the new Wing virtually maintenance-free by using hydraulically-adjusted valves and clutches, which meant the clutch and valves literally never needed to be adjusted. Combined with shaft drive and electronic ignition, these features meant that, under normal circumstances, the owner simply needed to add gasoline and occasionally change the oil to keep the bike on the road. Although long in use in the automotive world, combining all these labor-saving conveniences in one motorcycle was revolutionary in 1984.

Last of the Naked Wings

When Honda introduced the GL1200 for 1984, it also brought out a standard version of the bike. The company hadn't wanted to build such a machine, but just as in 1980, it succumbed to pressure from the aftermarket to build an undressed Gold Wing.

But, alas, it was too late for companies earning their keep by selling aftermarket fairings and luggage. People had become accustomed to store-bought touring bikes, and no longer were in the habit of rolling their own. Honda sold just a handful of the naked Wings, and dropped the standard version after just one year of production.

Regaining the Heavyweight Title

Honda sweetened the Gold Wing pot with a host of other improvements, too, such as increasing the

To survive the advent of the factory dresser, many aftermarket suppliers switched to selling chrome accessories and additional lighting for Gold Wings.

load capacity to 380 pounds, and increasing the carrying capacity of the luggage by 25 percent. The new seat, which still didn't earn universal praise, was generally considered an improvement over the GL1100. The press and the public did agree that this was the best Gold Wing ever.

The new Wing still wasn't perfect. While *Motorcyclist* admitted the suspension changes represented an improvement and that cornering clearance was increased, the editors still felt the bike could handle better. They especially disliked the new digital tachometer and speedometer because they were diffi-

Specials

Honda's been building special editions of the Gold Wing almost as long as it's been building Gold Wings. Honda imported its first limited edition Wing, the GL1000 LTD, to the United States in 1976. The differences between the LTD and the standard Wing were purely cosmetic. Candy-brown paint covered the LTD, accented by metallic-silver paint on the engine cases and high-quality chrome plating on the fenders and trim. Gold pinstriping matched the trick gold rims and spokes, and gold LTD badges along with a gold-stamped owners manual drove the golden theme home. A custom-quilted saddle coddled the lucky owner's hindquarters. Honda imported 2,000 of these bikes.

A much more rare Wing is the Executive, a Gold Wing sold in England in 1976. This bike featured a Rickman fairing and other touring accessories, and only 52 examples were sold. The Executive has the distinction of being the first fully-faired Gold Wing officially sold by Honda, predating the 1980 Interstate by four years.

Honda marketed another LTD version of the Gold Wing in 1985. Like its predecessor, this bike sported a variety of luxury features, such as a high-quality stereo with Dolby noise-reduction circuitry and four speakers, cruise control, an auto-leveling rear suspension that adjusted ride height according to the load, and a computerized dash that featured an electronic travel computer.

Unlike its predecessor, the 1985 LTD featured some major mechanical changes, most notably electronic fuel injection. In theory, this feature should have improved the Gold Wing's throttle response, but in reality, it proved to have the opposite effect. The system was supposed to deliver fuel precisely by monitoring throttle position, intake vacuum, atmospheric pressure, and temperature, but instead it made the bike run rough and burn a lot of fuel. Part of the problem involved unreliable fuel quality—the system was very sensitive to the octane level of gasoline—and part of the problem involved the interfacing of the system's mechanical and electronic components.

Honda built another special edition Gold Wing in 1986, the GL1200 SEi, also a fuel-injected bike. Honda made some changes to the fuel-injection system for the SEi, but if anything, the SEi ran rougher than the LTD. Honda dropped the model the following year and didn't take another stab at building a fuel-injected motorcycle until it produced the VFR800 in 1998.

The SEi was really the last of the limited-edition Gold Wings. In 1990 Honda came out with the SE version of the GL1500, but SE stood for "special equipment," not "special edition." There was nothing limited about the new model's production. In 1995 Honda commemorated the Gold Wing's twentieth anniversary with fairing and trunk badges, but it placed those badges on every single Wing built that year, excluding the anniversary bikes from attaining limited edition status. It did the same with 2000 model year Wings, only this time the badges commemorated the bike's twenty-fifth anniversary. ∎

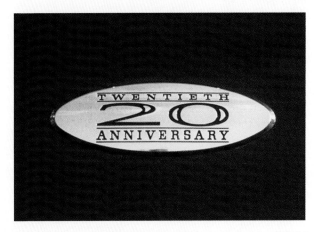

Honda commemorated the twentieth anniversary of Gold Wing production with special badges on all 1995 Gold Wings.

Mike Wright owns this stock (except for the windshield and case guards) 1976 GL1000 LTD. (photo by Nick Hoppner, courtesy Wing World)

Changes were more than skin deep on the fuel-injected GL1200 LTD of 1985. (photo courtesy Rider magazine)

Honda dealers in England sold only 52 Gold Wing Executives in 1976. (photo courtesy World's Motorcycles News Agency)

cult to read in high-speed situations, but in all honesty, this was more of a problem at the drag strip than in the real world. Other testers noted that the fuel gauge was as erratic as it had been on early versions of the GL1000, and that it was difficult to see the stereo controls at night. Many people noted that the seat still felt much less comfortable than the seats of the Wing's closest rivals, Yamaha's Venture and Kawasaki's six-cylinder ZN1300 Voyager. *Motorcyclist* complained of a mediocre horn and an optimistic speedometer. One tester commented on the messy-looking wires running down the left handlebar.

That list pretty much sums up most of the complaints leveled at the GL1200. Except for the uncomfortable seat, which was remedied via the aftermarket, the new Wing's problems were remarkably inconsequential. By building on the Wing's established strengths, Honda produced what, at the time, represented the closest thing to perfection a touring rider had ever seen. *Motorcyclist* wrote: "It has the same strengths as previous Gold Wings. The things they did well, it does better."

"This year the Honda engineers have pulled off an unbelievable trick," *Cycle* wrote. "They've taken a 790-pound machine and made it nimble and manageable."

The public responded to the GL1200 as enthusiastically as the press. The new Wing won out over Yamaha's Venture on the showroom floor and in the press. "The majority of the flaws in the Honda are gone now," *Motorcyclist* wrote. "The new-found handling quickness makes it easier and more enjoyable to ride than the big Venture . . . It seems that Yamaha's Venture had a very short stay at the top of the touring world."

Chapter 5

The Joy of Six

If It Ain't Broke . . .

During the Gold Wing's first decade, Honda scrambled to perfect their king of motorcycles, but with GL1200, it had come so close to perfection that the company now had a new problem: how to build a better-than-perfect Wing.

Not that there was a great public outcry for a better Gold Wing. There was increased competition, to be sure. In 1986, Suzuki introduced its Cavalcade, powered by the V-four engine from the company's Madura power cruiser, and Kawasaki brought out its Voyager XII, powered by an enlarged version of the Ninja's in-line four motor. Yamaha bumped the displacement of its Venture to 1300cc, but Honda's GL1200 still held its position atop the touring-bike heap. It seemed Honda had little incentive to improve its dominant Gold Wing.

But Honda's engineers had other plans. They knew that sooner or later someone would build a better tourer, and they never again wanted to be in the position of playing catch up. Strategy-wise, the next generation Gold Wing would be a preemptive strike. As good as the GL1200 was, Honda knew the flat-four engine was becoming obsolete.

The Resurrected M1

Ever since Project 371, rumors of six-cylinder Gold Wings had flourished. And ever since Shoichiro Irimajiri's team built the original M1, factions within the company had favored a six-cylinder production bike. When the GL1200 appeared, *Motorcyclist* commented on "rumors of a V-six design," but noted that Honda's surveys showed that owners

Opposite page

The GL1500, introduced in 1988, once again rewrote the book on luxury touring. (photo courtesy World's Motorcycles News Agency)

Left

Of all the competition the Gold Wing faced in the 80s, only Kawasaki's Voyager XII made it into the 21st century. (photo courtesy Kawasaki U.S.A.)

Right
Honda decided to go with the flat-six configuration in the GL1500 only after much internal debate. (photo courtesy World's Motorcycles News Agency)

Below left
The GL1500 set new standards for weather protection and comfort, for both rider and passenger.

Below right
When designing the GL1500's exhaust system, Honda sought to recreate the sound of a jet turbine.

favored a four because a six "wouldn't be a Gold Wing."

Many within Honda management shared that feeling. Engineers wanted a six, because they knew it would be difficult to get more power out of a four-cylinder engine without increasing vibration to intolerable levels; management, who worried about continuity and product recognition, favored a larger four.

Part of the goal of the new Gold Wing team formed in 1984, headed by Shigehisa Morinaka, was to figure out how much change Wingers were willing to accept. Based on the information gathered in the surveys mentioned in the *Motorcyclist* article, it appeared they might not be willing to accept very much change. Early design sketches reflect this conservatism, showing a bike that looked very much like the GL1500, except that it featured a 1300cc–1400cc flat four instead of a six. The first

mockup, built in the spring of 1985, also had a four-cylinder engine.

While this mockup was under construction, a group of engineers resurrected the flat-six engine from the old M1 test bike, installing it in a GL1200 frame. This test mule so impressed Honda management that, even though the styling of the next-generation Wing was in the final stages, they decided to make the new Gold Wing a flat-six instead of a flat-four.

The GL1500

The decision to go with a six-cylinder configuration was made in May of 1985. Within three years, the new GL1500 appeared in Honda showrooms. As with the GL1100 Interstate and the GL1000, the 1988 Gold Wing's statistics read like those of no other motorcycle before it: 1520cc flat-six engine, 66.9-inch wheelbase and an overall length of nearly

The GL1500 was the smoothest Wing yet, thanks to the rubber-mounted engine and the perfect primary balance of the flat-six architecture. (photo courtesy World's Motorcycles News Agency)

nine feet, 876 pounds when filled with 6.3-gallons of gas (finally a large enough tank!), and even a reverse drive.

The starter motor powered the slow-speed reverse drive. With the bike running and in neutral, the owner pulled a lever above the left-side cylinder bank, pressed the starter button, and the bike rolled backwards at a walking pace. Everyone who had ever paddled a Gold Wing backward up even the slightest incline appreciated this new feature.

A new fairing provided near-total protection from the elements. Rider comfort was further increased by moving the engine ahead 40mm, increasing rider leg room. To accomplish this,

Morinaka's team used a V-shaped radiator, to help clear the front tire.

Honda rubber mounted the new six-cylinder engine for additional smoothness. This proved necessary because, while the flat six had perfect primary balance, it had higher order imbalances that produced vibrations at certain rpm. Still, the engine was so smooth that there was no need for a heavy flywheel to smooth things out, as on the four. This helped the 1520cc powerplant rev more freely than had the old four-cylinder unit.

In spite of having a rubber-mounted engine, Honda claimed the new chassis was one-and-a-half times stiffer than the chassis on the GL1200. The

Though it weighed nearly 100 pounds more than its predecessor, the GL1500 proved to be more nimble. (photo courtesy World's Motorcycles News Agency)

The seat on the GL1500 represented many, many hours of hard work on the part of Honda's U.S. testing team.

Honda replaced the complex digital gauges used on the GL1200 with a set of conventional round dials on the GL1500.

seat was also improved. U.S. testers spent more time developing the seat than they had spent on any other single component, and their hard work paid off in the most comfortable seat ever mounted on a Gold Wing.

In addition to the obvious changes in style and engine architecture, the new Wing sported a number of detail changes. Honda abandoned the "Tokyo-by-night" video-game gauges used on the GL1200, reverting instead to less gimmicky and easier-to-read round dials. Only one rear shock held air—the other was conventional. The fork did retain Honda's TRAC anti-dive. The brakes remained linked, although the front discs were now squeezed by powerful twin-piston calipers. Three levers at the base of the trunk opened all the luggage compartments.

Honda engineers pulled out all stops to make the new Gold Wing the world's most refined touring motorcycle, studying details like the exhaust sound, trying to make them as pleasing as possible. The new Wing's three-section muffler strove to recreate the sound of a jet engine, since Honda's research showed that was a sound people enjoyed hearing.

Riders could enjoy all the fruits of Honda's research and study for $9,998.

On the Road

While motorcycle scribes had sacrificed entire forests praising the smoothness of previous iterations of the Gold Wing, nothing prepared them for the smoothness of the new six. Once again, the Wing sent them scrambling for new adjectives to describe the experience.

The new bike's nimble handling redefined what it meant to ride a huge motorcycle. In spite of reverting to 18-inch front and 16-inch rear wheels, the GL1500 felt even lighter and more flickable on the road than had the GL1200, even though it outweighed the smaller bike by 86 pounds. Even at a standstill, the big six-cylinder machine remained remarkably well balanced. Hoisting the GL1500 onto its centerstand was easier than hoisting up the earlier four-cylinder Wings.

The unified braking system was much improved from earlier versions, generating few complaints. Fuel mileage was acceptable, ranging from 35 to 40

***Above** The cockpit of the GL1500 provides one of the most luxurious perches from which to see the world. (photo courtesy American Honda/Vreeke & Associates)*

***Right, top to bottom** Initially offered only in a standard version, by 1991 buyers could chose between Interstate, Aspencade, and SE versions of the GL1500. (photo courtesy World's Motorcycles News Agency)*

miles per gallon, but dipping down into the mid-20s when the bike was pushed hard. Needless to say, most magazine test bikes turned in figures closer to the mid-20s than the mid-30s.

There were a few teething problems with the early GL1500s. 1988 and 1989 models occasionally suffered from jerky drivetrains, as well as intermittent problems with fork seals, brakes, electronic cruise control, windshield adjusters, and saddlebag seals, but all of these problems had been solved by 1990.

One Size Fits All

Honda made a major change for the 1988 model year by offering just one version of the Gold Wing—but that one model came with a list of features that left no one wanting. Each Gold Wing

came with a 24-watt-per-channel AM/FM radio cassette player, an electronic cruise control, a 546-watt AC generator, and a windscreen that could be raised or lowered without tools.

This approach lasted two years. In 1990, Honda introduced an SE version. Unlike the SEi of 1986, which stood for "Special Edition (injected)," this time the "SE" stood for "Special Equipment." The SE featured a vented windshield, adjustable passenger floorboards, a rear spoiler with a built-in brake light, illuminated stereo and cruise control switches, warm-air lower leg vents, two-tone paint, and cornering lights. It also gained 10 pounds, as well as a few dollars in price. The SE cost $13,498, compared to the standard Wing's $11,498 price tag.

In 1991, Honda reverted to offering the Gold Wing in three trim levels: Interstate, Aspencade,

One of the most noticeable changes for 1995 was the use of a chrome garnish on the front of the fairing.

Testers generally found the thinner seat used on the 1995-and-later GL1500s less comfortable than earlier versions, but as had always been the case, most owners mounted aftermarket seats, so few complained. (photo by Michael S. Biebrich)

and SE. The Aspencade came with the same level of equipment as the 1988 Gold Wing. The Interstate, a stripped model, jettisoned the cruise control, air compressor, and reverse drive. Such deletions helped bring the Interstate's wet weight down to 851.5 pounds, undercutting the SE's 890.5 wet weight by 39 pounds. It also brought the price tag down from $13,998 to $8,998, an incredible $5,000 difference.

Charting the Changes

Honda's GL1500 has enjoyed a remarkably long shelf life. The current version has been in production for thirteen seasons. All three four-cylinder models combined—the 1000, 1100, and 1200—were produced for a total of just thirteen seasons.

In all that time, very little has changed. The biggest changes occurred for the 1995 model year, the

Gold Wing's twentieth anniversary. The bulk of these changes centered around lowering the seat height, and it's debatable whether or not they were improvements. Heavier springs with less preload were used at both ends to lower ride height by half an inch, and the seat height was lowered another half inch by simply removing foam from the seat.

In its November 1994 test of a 1995 SE, *Cycle World* noted that these changes resulted in a tighter, more controllable ride on smooth roads, at the expense of composure on rougher roads. Editors also commented unfavorably on the thinner saddle, which they said compressed enough on a long day for a rider's buttocks to contact the seat pan on hard bumps. Overall, they said the 1995 Wing was less comfortable for long rides than earlier versions of the GL1500.

The Future

The GL1500 proved to be, finally, the king of motorcycles Shoichiro Irimajiri's team began working on in December of 1972. It was so good that just about all its competition literally gave up on the luxury-touring market. When Yamaha quit building the Venture after 1993, the only other big touring bikes left on the market were Harley's Electra Glide series and Kawasaki's Voyager XII, neither of which was really in the Gold Wing's class. While it's definitely a luxury-touring bike, Harley's Electra Glide Ultra classic competes in what is essentially a different market. The Voyager XII, while a fine bike in its own right, doesn't exactly compete head-to-head with the Gold Wing, either. It's main selling point is that it costs $3,200 less than the least expensive Gold Wing, and $5,600 less than a top-of-the-line SE.

In 1975 Honda stunned the motorcycling world by introducing a $2,899, 635-pound, four-cylinder bike that featured an astonishing 60.5-inch wheelbase. Twenty-five years later Honda's $17,599, 920-pound, six-cylinder motorcycle, with its 66.9-inch wheelbase and reverse drive is not an oddity—it's the industry standard.

Although Harley-Davidson has always built its own interpretation of luxury touring bikes, in many ways, the Electra Glide competes in a different market than the Gold Wing.

In 1999, BMW's K1200LT gave the Gold Wing something it hadn't had in nearly twenty years: serious competition.

Clockwise, top left Honda's X-Wing gives a glimpse into the Gold Wing's future. *(photo courtesy* Motorcyclist *magazine)*

Lower left The X-Wing's 150-degree V-six will power the first Gold Wing of the new Millennium. *(photo courtesy* Motorcyclist *magazine)*

Lower middle and right Expect futuristic styling on the next generation Gold Wing. *(photos courtesy* Motorcyclist *magazine)*

As good as it is, the Gold Wing is about to undergo its next major change. Even if the competition had remained dormant, the Wing would have changed, simply because "new" sells, but the competition hasn't remained dormant. When BMW introduced its excellent K1200LT in 1999, Honda's ultimate motorcycle began losing magazine comparison tests for the first time in nearly two decades.

Honda has remained elusive about future plans, but sources connected with the company say Honda's original plan was to introduce an 1800cc version of the current flat-six Gold Wing for the 1999 model year, and introduce an all-new bike in 2005. But the introduction of BMW's K1200LT may have changed that plan. Other sources say that when Honda learned of the new Beemer, it realized that its new Wing had to not only equal the K1200LT, but surpass it. Management wanted to take no chances this time, so they accelerated development of the 2005 bike, moving the introduction date up to 2001.

What will the new bike be like? As of this writing, no one knows exactly what the machine will look like, but we do know a few things about the future Wing, based on Honda's X-Wing concept bike, shown in the fall of 1999.

We can expect obvious changes, such as all-new styling. After all, the GL1500's bodywork was crafted in the mid-1980s, back in a time when computer-aided design equipment was much cruder than it is today. The new Wing will definitely look the part of a 21st-century luxury tourer. And it will most likely feature the X-Wing's multi-adjustable ergonomics, an area where BMW has done much pioneering work. Expect it to feature all the luxury items for which BMW is known, such as heated grips, heated seats, CD changer, electrically-adjusted windshield, perhaps even an in-trunk beverage cooler.

The 150-degree V-six engine from the X-Wing is also a distinct possibility for the new Gold Wing.

The Valkyrie

In the spring of 1996, Honda released the Valkyrie, a high-powered cruiser built around the flat-six engine of the GL1500. The Valkyrie pumps out more horsepower than any other stock, mass-produced cruiser, thanks to a number of hot-rodding changes to the basic Wing engine. Gone are the GL's hydraulically adjusted valves, replaced with solid units that need adjustment. Like the M1 before it, the GL1500 gets by with just two downdraft carburetors, in this case a pair of 32mm diaphragm-type carbs. And also like the M1, those carbs feed into three-into-one intake manifolds that are shrouded with water jackets to keep the fuel-charge temperature constant. The Valkyrie uses six downdraft carbs, and uses them to good effect. The Valkyrie Interstate *Motorcyclist* tested in August of 1999 cranked out 97.1 horsepower at the rear wheel.

The Valkyrie comes in three versions—standard, Tourer, and Interstate. The standard comes sans luggage and fairing, making it the closest thing to a naked Gold Wing available to the public since 1984. The Tourer adds a pair of hard saddlebags and a large clear windshield. The Interstate is a genuine touring bike, with an Electra Glide-esque handlebar-mounted fairing and a complete set of luggage with a top case. ■

Without its bodywork, the Valkyrie looks like it could be a six-cylinder version of the old naked Wing. (photo courtesy World's Motorcycles News Agency)

Top left

The Valkyrie scraps the two carbs and hydraulically-adjusted valves of the Gold Wing in its quest for more power. (photo courtesy American Honda/Vreeke & Associates)

Top right

One look at these pipes and you know this bike packs six slugs.

Left

In its soul, the Valkyrie is a pure hot rod.

Top *The standard Valkyrie comes without any bodywork, stripping the cruiser experience to its bare essentials. (photo courtesy World's Motorcycles News Agency)*

Middle *The Valkyrie Tour adds a windshield and a pair of hard saddle bags to the Valkyrie formula. (photo courtesy World's Motorcycles News Agency)*

Bottom *In 1999, Honda revived the Interstate name, affixing it to the full-dress touring version of the Valkyrie. (photo courtesy American Honda/Vreeke & Associates)*

While a V-six engine might seem like sacrilege to some Wingers, the concept has merit. By angling the cylinder banks upward, designers create more room for the rider's feet. Besides, the cylinder banks will each only be angled up fifteen degrees from horizontal, so the Wing's greatest feature, its low center of gravity, will remain.

Most of all, you can expect the new Gold Wing to build on its predecessors' strengths and improve on its weaknesses. Wingers ready acceptance of the six-cylinder Wing means they value function over tradition, and if the new engine works better than the old, you can expect them to embrace the new machine, at least as long as it continues the tradition Gold Wing riders expect: the tradition of constant improvement.

Appendix A

Buying a Used Wing

Over the years Gold Wings have earned a well-deserved reputation for quality, and have been very reliable bikes. Generally, when buying a used Gold Wing you'd look for the same things you would when buying any other used motorcycle: condition, maintenance logs, mileage, and whether it's been wrecked and rebuilt. But there are a couple of exceptions.

The most infamous problem with Gold Wings has been stator failure on four-cylinder bikes. This is an especially expensive problem on Wings because you have to pull the engine to get at the stator, which resides within the engine cases.

Prevailing theory blames the failure on an inexpensive electrical plug between the stator and the rest of the electrical system. The sole purpose of this plug was to ease the installation of the engine on the assembly line. Once the bike rolled off the line, the plug served no further purpose.

Former *Wing World* editor and current Senior Editor at *Motorcycle Consumer News* Fred Rau, an electrical engineer by trade, has owned more Gold Wings than he can shake a stick at, and he said every bike he's seen with a stator problem has had corrosion on that plug. The problem is that the dielectric grease washes out of the plastic connector over time and the metal connections inside become corroded. Corroded connectors create resistance, which confuses the stator and makes it ramp up to full output. This is what causes it to fail. Fred said that in his experience, cutting the plug and hard wiring the stator into the electrical system has proven 100 percent effective at curing stator problems.

The plug is located behind the left-side engine cover. There you'll find three yellow wires coming out of the back of the engine block and going into a white nylon connector. If those connections are corroded, you'll probably have an expensive stator repair in your near future. You can test the stator by starting the bike and checking all three wires with a multimeter. You should have almost the exact same output on all three wires, around 14.2 volts. If any one is different from the others, one of the coils in the three-phase stator is starting to short out.

If the wires have been cut and the nylon connector has been removed, let out a sigh of relief, because this stator has already been replaced by someone who knows the scoop.

There's really no good reason for not hard-wiring the stator, even if your connections aren't corroded and your stator is working correctly. Some dealers won't warranty a stator if the connection has been cut and hard-wired, but if that's the case, you simply need to find a better dealer. Chances are that someone who'd try to weasel out of that couldn't be trusted for much else, either.

The stator seems to be most problematic on the GL1200, probably because that bike had more electrical equipment and placed more of a load on the stator than did the GL1000 or GL1100.

If a rider abused a GL1000, he or she could fry clutches fairly quickly, but chances are most people owning such bikes today aren't using them for smoky burnouts or for running through the quarter mile. Under extreme abuse, the GL1000 was known to snap its crankshaft on occasion.

Worn rear splines can constitute another expensive repair on pre-1988 Gold Wings. The original shaft-drive system of the GL1000, which was used until 1987, was not designed for a touring bike. Pulling trailers can be especially damaging to the shaft splines. To check the splines, put the bike on its centerstand and see if the rear wheel moves side to side or front to back. If it moves, it could mean the bike has badly worn splines. If that's the case, it would be worthwhile to remove the wheel and inspect the hub before buying the bike, even if you have to pay a mechanic to do the work. Repairing splines is an expensive proposition, costing up to $1,000, or even more. Once you purchase a four-cylinder Gold Wing, you should check the splines at least every 30 to 40 thousand miles.

A couple of specific models, the 1985 LTD and the 1986 SEi, could cause you headaches. If you buy one of these bikes, make certain the computerized instruments work, because if they fail, they are unrepairable and unreplaceable. If you have such a bike and the instruments aren't working, you could try pulling out the instrument modules and cleaning the copper knife-edge connectors with a pencil eraser or a Scotchbrite pad. You can also do this to the stereos on earlier Interstates and Aspencades.

About the only thing you really need to check on a GL1500 is whether or not it was recalled for the bank-angle sensor. This is a sensor that killed the engine if the bike tipped over. The problem was that sometimes it killed the engine while the bike was leaned over in a fast turn, causing riders to crash. Call the National Highway Traffic Safety Association's hotline (888-327-4236) to make sure the recall was performed.

As for the regular things you'd look for on a used motorcycle, realize that Wingers often have very different ideas of what constitutes low mileage than, say, owners of Suzuki GSX-Rs. While many sportbikes seldom see the far side of 30,000 miles, 50,000 or even 60,000 is a reasonably low figure for a Gold Wing. If the bike has been properly maintained (and if the stator is strong and the splines are in good condition), such figures should pose no problem. Lower miles are always better, but Wingers regularly get 100–200,000 miles from their bikes.

Appendix B

Gold Wing Resources

Gold Wings are more than just motorcycles—they are a motorcycle culture, a claim only a handful of bikes can make with any legitimacy. Like any motorcycle culture, a separate world has grown around Honda's popular touring bike, a world with resources invaluable to Gold Wing owners.

The most obvious Gold Wing-specific resources are the many clubs devoted to the Wing. The largest of these, the Gold Wing Road Riders Association (GWRRA), is also the world's largest single-marque club. GWRRA membership provides a wide array of benefits, not the least of which is the club's terrific magazine, *Wing World*. You can contact the GWRRA at: http://www.gwrra.org.

While the GWRRA is the largest Gold Wing club, there are many other fine organizations devoted to the Wing, clubs like the Gold Wing Touring Association (GWTA), an international not-for-profit organization of touring motorcyclists. The GWTA welcomes riders of all types of motorcycles, but members mostly ride Gold Wings. You can reach the GWTA at: http://www.gwta.org.

Another terrific and entertaining resource is Wings On The Internet (WOTI), a mailing list for people interested in Gold Wings. The level of knowledge WOTI members possess is truly amazing. You can contact WOTI at: http://www.armchair.mb.ca/wings/.

An interesting organization that is not specifically a Gold Wing group is the Guardian Whales. The Guardian Whales were formed after the death of Australian rider Erold Ansell. While touring the United States aboard his Gold Wing, Erold accidentally veered into the left lane and was killed by an oncoming pickup truck. From this accident was born the Guardian Whales International Motorcycle Rider Support Group, a volunteer group that accompanies motorcyclists traveling in foreign lands, assisting them until they learn local traffic laws and patterns. Groups like this are typical of the kind of decent people you meet when you hang around with Wingers. If you're interested in becoming a Guardian Whale, you can contact them at: http://guardianwhales.cx.

Index

About the Author

Darwin caught the motorcycle bug at the age of five, when his cousin brought home a shiny new Honda CB350. He supports his lifelong motorcycle habit by any means necessary. He's worked as a factory laborer, farm hand, truck driver, potato inspector, editor, newspaper reporter, and adjunct professor, teaching journalism, technical writing, and composition. He currently works as a freelance writer and editor in the Minneapolis area. He also mans the illustrious Midwest Desk for *Motorcyclist* magazine. He's been riding since the ripe old age of 11, and he has logged at least 25,000 motorcycle miles each year for the past 15 years. His dream garage contains a Ducati 750SS (Roundcase, with a duck-egg blue frame), Series C Vincent Rapide, Moto Guzzi V11 Sport, KTM Adventurer, Honda VFR800 Interceptor, and 1993 Gold Wing SE. His real garage is somewhat more spartan.

Darwin Holmstrom is also the author of *The Complete Idiot's Guide to Motorcycles* (with some assistance from the editors of *Motorcyclist* magazine). This is his second book.

(photo by Brian J. Nelson)